Our Lucky Day

Helen Bethune

Illustrated by Xiangyi Mo and Jingwen Wang

Contents

Billy's Journal

Thursday, June 17

We've been living and working on the gold-mining fields for almost six months now. We moved here from back east to make our fortune.

I sure do wish we could find gold! Every night, while Pa makes a new leg for a chair or something, he says, "Tomorrow, Ma, that'll be the day I find gold."

Mr. Rose, the goldsmith back east, found gold when he came here. Then he went home and made it into jewelry. He sold it to all the rich people in town.

Pa hopes to make his fortune one day, too.

Since we've been out here in California, all I seem to do is chores. I fetch water from the stream. I find firewood. I chop kindling.

Annie, my older sister, looks after our little sisters. She helps Ma with the washing and the mending, too.

Our clothes are so shabby. We have to scrub them on the rocks by the river to get them clean. Now they have holes in them.

Pa's pants are falling apart. Ma has used up almost all her thread and material patching our clothes.

If only we could find gold. Everything would be so much better then.

Friday, June 18

There aren't many plates and cups in our cabinet anymore. Annie sometimes breaks them when it's her turn to wash dishes.

Today Ma sent us to Mr. Lee's pottery store to buy new ones. We saw the special ovens they use when they make the clay plates and cups.

Mr. Lee was glad to see us. Pa built shelves in Mr. Lee's store a few months ago.

"Your Pa is an excellent carpenter," he said.

Tonight, Pa looked so tired. I told him what Mr. Lee had said. That made him smile.

Still no gold, though. Maybe tomorrow will be our lucky day.

9

Saturday, June 19

Ma said she is tired of having to mend Pa's pants every day.

We went to Mr. Cooper's dry-goods store today. Ma was looking for some tough material to use to make new pants. Mr. Cooper had a whole new load of rough canvas for wagon covers and tents.

Ma bought some of this canvas cloth to use for Pa's pants. She is a dressmaker, so she knows about material. She said that canvas might be good for making gold miners' pants, because it's such a strong fabric.

I'm beginning to think Pa will never find gold, no matter what kind of pants he wears.

Monday, June 21

Annie and I went to Farmer Kelly's farm to see what vegetables he had for sale.

Farmer Kelly told us that more and more people are moving here each day. They all need fresh vegetables. He says growing or making goods that people need is the best way to make money. He says that we will never get rich looking for gold.

Maybe he's right.

13

Across the road, Mr. Towie has set out hives among the trees. He's starting up a *bee* farm. Soon the town will have lots of honey for people to buy.

Ma had a surprise for Pa when he got home from work today. She'd started to make him some new pants out of the canvas cloth from Mr. Cooper's store.

She got annoyed when Annie and I played tug-of-war with some of the cloth. We were showing how tough it was.

It was the most fun we've had in a long time.

15

Tuesday, June 22

Pa had a day off from looking for gold today. Mr. Cooper needed Pa to build bigger shelves in his store. I helped him.

Goods from the east come in by wagon train almost every day, so Mr. Cooper needs more storage space.

Ma asked Pa to buy buttons, ribbons, thread, and needles from Mr. Cooper's store. She uses those things to make dresses.

17

Tonight, Pa said, "Mr. Cooper is making a lot of money selling things. Maybe we should start our own business."

Ma seemed very happy to hear Pa say that.

It seems to me that starting a business could be a good idea. That's the way some people here are finding their fortunes. Their money is coming from people like us—the people buying the things that they're selling.

Pa and Ma weren't making much money back east. But they could make money here. This town needs carpenters and dressmakers.

I think they should open their own stores!

19

Wednesday, June 23

Ma finished Pa's new canvas pants last night. He wore them today.

When he came back from work, his pants looked as good as new, but Pa's legs surely didn't. They were red and sore, because the canvas was so rough.

Pa said he would have to keep wearing his old, worn-out pants. So Ma patched his old pants some more.

The idea of finding our fortune out here seems further away than ever today.

Thursday, June 24

Today Mr. Cooper gave Pa some new pants for helping him build those shelves on Tuesday. I got a pair, too.

These pants are made of really tough cotton. It's almost as tough as canvas, but not as stiff and rough. Mr. Cooper said the material is called "denim." Someone had a good idea when they decided to use denim to make pants.

Ma really likes the new pants. Pa and I do, too!

23

Friday, June 25

Today Pa and I actually found some gold!

I went with Pa to help him at the stream. We wore our new denim pants. We had been panning and sifting for a little while when I saw some shining specks in the bottom of my pan. I called Pa to come and see.

"Our denim pants have made us lucky!" I cried, as Pa gazed at the specks of gold.

"I think you're right, Billy!" he said. "This may be our lucky day!"

We looked and looked for the rest of the day, but we didn't find any more gold.

"Billy found some gold!" Pa told Ma and the girls when we got home.

Ma gave me a big hug, and the girls all wanted to see the gold. Then, after supper, Ma and Pa talked for a long time. They looked really happy.

Today was the best day we've had in a long time!

Sunday, September 27

It's been more than three months now since I've written in my journal.

We're still living on the gold fields. But Pa went back to being a carpenter, and Ma took up dressmaking again.

We didn't make our fortune with the specks of gold we found. But Pa makes quite a lot of money building houses and furniture.

Best of all, our lucky denim pants gave Ma a good idea. She makes strong denim pants. She sells them to lots of miners and other workers.

I guess Farmer Kelly was right. Growing or making goods that people need is the best way to make money.

Mr. Lee, Mr. Cooper, and Mr. Towie found their fortune that way. And now, so have we!

The History of Jeans

In the story, Pa and Billy wear strong denim pants when they are looking for gold. Pants like these were the first jeans.

The first person to sell denim jeans to gold miners was Levi Strauss. He and his business partner made strong jeans. They put metal studs or rivets on the corners of pockets to stop the fabric from tearing.

These gold miners are wearing jeans.

Think About the Story

In *Our Lucky Day*, Billy and his family hope to make their fortune in the gold fields. Think about these questions.

- Billy and his dad are each given denim pants. How were these pants different from other pants?

- Billy and his family meet many different people in the story. What goods do these people produce?

- How do Billy and his family make their fortune in the end?

To learn more about how some goods are produced, read the books below.

SUGGESTED READING
Windows on Literacy
Cotton Comes From Plants
Wool Keeps Me Warm